SILHOUETT

A BOOK OF

Roge... ...

Quanaah Publishing

www.quanaah-publishing.com

Silhouettes of the Soul
©Copyright 2013

Written by Roger A. Talley and Rhonda C. Bivins
Edited by S. Quanaah, Asia M. Jackson, and D. Scott
Cover Design by Kevin Bivins, S. Quanaah, and Roger A. Talley

Dedication

My biggest inspiration goes to Rhonda C. Bivins "Rhon" for all your creativity, support, understanding and love, without whom none of this would be possible.

A special dedication in loving memory of my father Howard L. Talley and wonderful sister Christina Talley who continue to encourage and inspire me from heaven's throne.

Acknowledgement

Love truly began with a prayer and from that moment on I have been able to enjoy love and all its splendors and encounters. Without those events in my life I would still be looking for love instead of writing about it.

Home for me is Rhonda, Arsha, Monique, Michia and Cortez, it is where I feel the warmth of their love and I am blessed and grateful.

A special acknowledgement to my mother: Ever Talley, who has shown me the real strength in life and love and to never lose confidence in it.

Gus T., Jay R., Reggie A., Mike S., Eric B., Tommy P., and Brian D. for all your brotherly love and advice.

I am indebted to S. Quanaah of Quanaah Publishing, Asia M. Jackson of Afflatus Press Publishing, and Author D. Scott for their professional influences and editorial assistance, Thank you for believing.

Thank You!

Roger A. Talley

Table of Contents

Silhouettes of the Soul

Freestyling
"Midnight Message"

Dark is the night but your beauty shines through like the sun on stain-glass windows or morning dew, as we laugh and talk to show our heartfelt thoughts. Beaming and gleaming about the life we've now sought.

Essence so sweet, body so divine this passion will last a whole lifetime for persistence and strength is what you exemplify, spoken words of intent honest and genuine. More than you think you are, less than you aspire to be, together with love, strength and support let's soar high above the trees.

Unlikely suspect to capture my eye, with the charm of a black knight in disguise, test after test I've proven I'm the best, your heart I will capture; not like the rest.

My traps you've evaded this I must attest, still being criminal my heart you still seek to arrest. Freedom of expressions, creativity of our minds, paper and pen describes our hearts desire, so arrest yes but not to lock away, for free is your spirit in every way.

Free like a bird you've exclaimed me to be capturing, cultivating a well-defined destiny.
Majestic and dignified on destiny's road, still you motivate, inspire as we rise higher in thoughts, life, love ...

A phenomenal woman you've helped reveal and true passion is the essence of what I truly conceal. Conceal it not my phenom, it's not the passion, but the pure ecstasy that will be revealed.

Ecstasy pure and felt all the time, with every thrust, ever movement a majestic moment in time. The midnight hour, we've found our time, a prayer to strengthen our spiritual side. Lord, guard and keep us throughout the night, until we rise in morning light.

We've listed the pros and weighed the cons, never to trade for the 20 our 80 of a lifetime!

A Symbol

Every moment with you is kept frozen in my

mind,

Your beauty and spirit overwhelms me, for there is more to

you than your physical form.

The energy and essence of your presence compels, elevate,

and motivates every fiber of my being in every way.

Beautiful, soulful, royal, mystic and strong,

Like a red rose ... a gift from above ... the symbol

of Love.

Acknowledgement

Your intelligence and creativity

is like amazing grace, how sweet it is …

Your voice soothing,

Like nana's lullaby and your beauty captivates making you

wondrous to behold.

Your heart and how you make me feel when sharing time

and space,

Is like floating on a cloud, heavenly …

If passion, desire, beauty, intellect and creativity had an

image to copy, it would be you!

Beauty to Me

Your wisdom is surpassed by your beauty
Your beauty by your inner spirit which comes from GOD
above,

Knowing that beauty is a gift from GOD and there's
nothing that makes its way more directly into the soul than a
gift from GOD…

You are beauty, and in my soul
This is a blessing to me.

Blessings

Family ... Blessing,

Time ... Blessing,

Sharing ... Blessing,

You ... Blessing,

Me ... Blessing,

Life ... Blessing,

Love ... Blessing,

Togetherness ... Blessing,

Spiritual Growth ...

Blessing,

These are the blessings we recognize, but the true blessing

is the one GOD has put inside us; the spirit that won't be

denied.

Comfort, Peace, Assurance and Love,

all gifts from GOD above ...

You are my gift and blessing!

Timeline

Today …

The here and now for you and me

Tomorrow …

What will be our hopes and dreams brought into reality.

Yesterday …

In my heart forever under lock and key

Weeks …

How the time passes so effortlessly.

Months …

Give way to knowledge, growth and more possibilities.

Years …

Our lifelong journey into eternity

Each dream now reality with GOD, love, life and family.

Take …

This walk along with me,

walk this timeline and fulfill our destiny.

Can't Wait

Excitement,

desire,

anticipation fills my mind

Waiting,

longing,

thinking about seeing you one more time!

Unexpected

Spoken words a delight to hear,
Excitement and desire grows without fear.
Desires into a throbbing passion
Lead to an uncontrollable escapade full of fire.
Bliss once, twice, three times so nice;
Friendship, companionship, partnership
And a sensual sexual ecstasy
Found in the least likely suspect ... Me

Chance Meeting

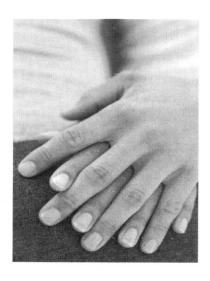

A once meeting by chance now regular happenstance,

Separate lives are becoming one,

Clear title distinctions and we both know why,

Nothing beats failure like a good honest try.

Try because you can, try 'cause you must, convince me

once more….

This is love not lust.

Mesmerized

Mesmerized by it all,

Your sultry soul sends sensations through my mind

The creativity of your mental chambers is like being at the

gates of heaven

Longing to savor your essence so sweet

Wetness on my tongue

Constantly flowing with positive energy

knowledge, wisdom, understanding, love, peace and

happiness represents the unselfish phenom that is you …

Mesmerized by it all!

In God We Trust

This love is blessed with goodness and grace,

HE allows us to see it own one another face.

Our words give power to create and inspire, our hearts give way to passion and desire.

Dream what we may, do what we must, put it all in HIS hands…

For in God we trust!

My Johnathan

Waiting, anticipating, maintaining, sustaining life,
and family
Oh Johnathan, my Johnathan where could he be?
An illusion before you that was never to be,
Temporary pleasures, find hidden treasures,
My Johnathan…oh could this be?
Excitement, desire, passion, intrigue, spirit and love, are a
few of his gifts God sent from above.
Possibilities now realities, make life more complete
knowing that HE has placed Johnathan
Right here at my feet.

The Escapade

Anticipation throughout the day of what the evening would
bring...

Dinner, Red Cat and total ecstasy.

1-2-3 intensely we climb

4 brings tears of pure ecstasy that blows our minds

5 exploding into reality the love between you and me.

Energy exhausted,

Bodies drenched,

Sensual moans

Is all that is left

Unspoken words, caressing of souls

Now this love making escapade

just has to be told...

The Course

Rise we will do if but just from our beds

Encouraged,

motivated,

loved and spiritually fed.

Each moment we steal is a stepping stone for our lives to

have and hold dearly, leaving no one deprived.

Every area of excellence... we have yet to discover

Providing love,

support and faith;

we'll build up one another.

Stay the course with me, I'll ride it through with you, this

my love, the fool proof plan...

Written, to be proven, tried and all true!

R.C.B.

Striving

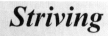

To awake with beauty, love and grace,
Compassion shown in every giving detail
down to the food on our plates.

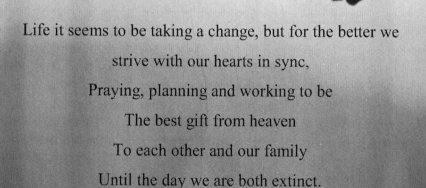

Life it seems to be taking a change, but for the better we
strive with our hearts in sync,
Praying, planning and working to be
The best gift from heaven
To each other and our family
Until the day we are both extinct.

Love

Curiosity that serenades the soul

Spiritual and mental connections

Mesmerizing and nourishing our growth

Hearts longing to be caressed by an illusion seldom reached

Divinity's creative force bonding us through eternity

Passionate encounters, sensual escapades

Bare-bodies embracing lead us to say

What is love?

Love is heart, mind, body, soul and spirit

All giving trade-offs to the wondrous freedoms

Justice and equalities that God has giving us as the gift …

Love!

Praise

Rise and shine in the morning light

praising God for this life.

Formulating thoughts of my coco colored queen; beautiful,

radiant, majestic, the reflection of life.

Knowledge and wisdom gives way to our hearts delights;

true love now in our sight.

God has touched each spirit in his own special way; to

nourish, lead, love, and support each other in every way.

You Are

The very essence of beauty is what shines through, so loving, affectionate in all you do.

Mind so strong, heart of gold, spirit touched by God; this we both know.

Life characteristics and attributes make you so unique that no adequate words can explain your strength, but for all your strength and pride, deeper inside is your greatest prize and it makes you wonderful and beautiful.

Dedication

Black woman you are:
Mother, lover, friend, teacher, provider, maintainer and supporter, the true bond of life.

Black woman you are:
The sweet manifestation of beauty that creates a loving atmosphere.

Black woman you are:
The joy, inspiration and pride of you,
And I'm open, honest and true
it lets me know that I wouldn't - I couldn't be without you.

Black woman you are:
So much more than a physical treat that brings our urges pleasure; pass the surface of what is deeper to the inner core, is where your true beauty will be revealed.

Black woman you are:

20.

Beautiful, graceful, the evolution of creativity. Intelligent, exciting, intriguing, dignifying and self-reliant, man's reality not to be characterized ... Simply.

Black woman you are:
The presence I recognize from heaven, with your beautiful brown skin, piercing eyes, magnetic attraction and graceful smile; your energy and spirit compels me.

Black woman you are:
Exemplary everyday with all that you are
Hope and desire to become and every time I see, talk, hold, sleep, wake and pray with you
I realize that our love is a true blessing.

Black Woman You Are ...
Black Woman You Just Are.

Elevated

Beautiful on the outside,

An expression of what's in your heart

Smart, creative and funny are your expression in thought.

Affection, protection, passion, love are enjoyed by your
touch,

You, me, we, us ... Elevated!

Empowered Words

Love, peace, honor, truth, courage and dignity

are the characteristics received from you,

Your love gives peace; peace elevates honor and that honor

demands truth;

truth in love gives courage;

courage builds dignity;

dignity allows your true love and character to shine through;

character is what God has given you.

Powerful descriptive words of admiration and gratitude

filled with love,

for the spirit and essence that is a blessing to be shared with

you.

Silky Chocolate Tea

Steaming hot like a warm summer night

Black in color is my delight

Honey or sugar makes your essence

sweeter in my mind

To taste your wetness … Mmmm pure ecstasy

Ancient wisdom has brought you through time pouring

positive energy, knowledge, and elevating minds

If I could pour a little of you into me,

Silky Chocolate Tea is what we would be

Reality Check

Reality check …

1, 2, 3 thoughts of you and I,

Filled with hopes and possibilities

Conversations once on hold,

now spoken into reality

Realization of growth through love and spirituality,

no longer filled with guilt,

just the desires of what can be

Providing what is needed for family,

love, life, and spirit;

this helps us grow together

Blessed… infinitely.

IT

We think about IT, sing about IT, dream about IT, we even lose sleep worrying over IT, when we don't know we have IT we search for IT, when we discover IT, we don't know what to do with IT and we fear losing IT.

IT: is a constant source of pleasure and pain, even though we don't know which IT will be from one moment to the next.

IT: is easy to spell and hard to define and IT is impossible to live without.

IT: is Love …

All of mine to you!!

Instructions

"Simplicity is one of the keys to life and love"

Give her two roses each with a note;

Rose One: *"For The Woman I Love"*

Rose Two: *"For My Best Friend."*

Morning Fire

Fueled by passion, driven by desire, an explosion of

ecstasy...

Morning Fire.

Sensual caressing elevating into melodic moans, unleashing

the sweet sensations of your treasure chest ...

Morning Fire.

Minds and bodies fully engaged with growing intensity,

increasing your wondrous

wet silkiness ...

Morning Fire.

Passion, desire, rapture and bliss fuels the love held deep

inside bringing fourth

our pure ecstasy ...

Morning Fire.

Craftsmen

God gave each and every one of us the tools needed

to make it through this life.

Each of us are craftsmen

We all just have to know what it is we are building!

Say What?

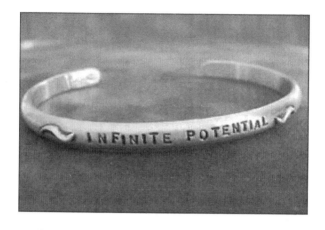

They Say: You can't

I Say: You can.

They Say: What If?

I Say: What if I show you opportunity and growth - never doubt?

They Say: When will?

I Say: When will the choice we make reflect our plans and we realize that hard work and dedication are the only choices.

They Say: How will?

I Say: By trusting and believing in God, self, family and your whole support system.

They Say: Who are you?
I Say: One person striving to be all I can for the service of God, family and community, no more, no less.

They Say: Why?
I Say: Because it is time for us all to stop, make a choice, and take a stand for something and/or someone greater than ourselves and lead our life by HIS example.

They Say: What's in it for you?
I Say: The ability to grow and understand that the more I become with God, life, love, family and community the more I can positively effect change in my and someone elses life and circumstance.

Black & White Soirée

Reflections of you in my mind; poised, elegant, graceful and so refined, flooded images that made me wish I could be that beautiful black dress, a vision so divine.

Excitement, direction, new possibilities guiding the careers, hopes, aspirations from the potential of who's who in this society.

So hand in hand and heart to heart we trust in each other and God above, our paths been laid and our niche will be found, with HIM guiding... there's no stopping us now!

You Are Loved

Warmth and grace forever seen in your face,

Your love and passion penetrates and caress my soul from

every touch which creates the desire to love you more with

each breath.

Voice; soothing, strong, compassionate, and motivating all

in one melodic tone.

Soulful, majestic, dignified, attractive physically and

mentally -making your beauty the standard for all to behold.

Heart and spirit blessed from above, my God sent gift…

You Are Loved!!

Pray

I Pray

For an abundant life.

I Pray

That our hearts remain united as God designed them to be.

I Pray

For an increase in each one of us and our family.

I Pray

That God's blessings forever guide our possibilities.

I Pray

For a change in spirit, life, love and humanity.

I Pray

That together we will achieve peace, comfort

and security.

I Pray

For a better tomorrow.

I Pray

For an eternity of love and growth with you.

I Pray

You Pray

We Pray ... Together!

Morning Delights

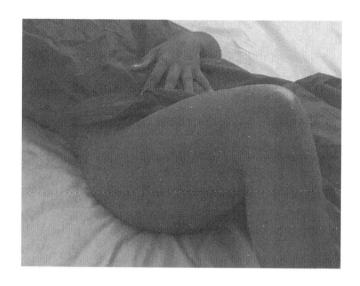

I'm held spellbound

Throbbing, caressing, a sensual escapade

Held in moans, unbridled passion in the early dawn.

Lost in the ardor of you and I

Peaks the ecstasy as time slips by

Realizing love is much more intense with you

Especially during the time period: between dawn and noon.

Morning delights!

Inspired Love

Inspired, you captivated my very soul

All that I am, all I had hope to be,

I will become with you

A reflection of you is the love between us.

Thankful and grateful I am

To be experiencing the life,

love and the gravity of you …

Family, happiness and unconditional love

Inspired by you.

Comfort in Love

You are the light that shines through the darkest night; the voice that comforts to let me know everything's going to be alright; the heart that reaches out giving love, compassion, and support; So hug me; love me and keep me in your care and I vow to always be here, to honor, love, and respect you from now until eternity; You are the console of life.

Cocoa Brown Skin

Cocoa brown skin delight… captivating spirit, essence irresistible, your expression of self, love, family and equality transcends reality; you elevate, stimulate cultivate… you are my cocoa brown skin delight.

Intellect, creativity and beauty effortlessly flowing simultaneously forming the highest standards of what love, peace and happiness in this life should be… you are my cocoa brown skin delight.

Mother, friend, counselor, lover, partner and companion through the highs and lows, your heart pours out knowledge, wisdom and understanding making you forever true to each title and never demanding… You are my cocoa brown skin delight.

Experiencing all that life has to give, binding of hearts, filling of souls beautiful and precious blessings from God above, divine intervention entrusted to us from eternity to infinity our love will last… my cocoa brown skin delight

Now I See

Now I See...

All the possibilities and dreams of freedoms and equality hoped for by every man before me.

Now I See...

Brought and taught enslaved mentally and physically, blood into the mother earth; but spirits unbroken transcend those rights and wrongs.

Now I see...

How I was supposed to be perceived; slave, property, a reflection of humanity, used by trickery to further deceive and strip away my History... so that I would be His-Story.

Now I See...

The knowledge of my past as the fuel to my future; knowing one's true self allows understanding of my origin and who I am… Kings!

Now I See…

As I search for equality, starting back from the Mississippi, Alabama days of old until I find that America might be blind, as I see a reflection of me, controlling what was never to be…

President Barack Obama.

Now I See…

That which was most feared from the start; ideas, perseverance, character of heart, the God giving spirit, knowledge and justice and it's that past that guides our future and will lead us to a better tomorrow.

Now I See…

It all had to be, this is our reality. Brought no more as property, no broken heart or spirits consumed by trickery, no longer taught in the fields of old, now teachers of many in universities;

Now I See,

Do You See… your reality started with me!

Evolution into a Man

Filled with the desire to be, the Man, partner, companion, mentor, the lead, and using truth, understanding, compassion, and experience as my guide; with God the Holy Spirit and the angels by my side I strive to take a boy to a Man

Love of self, life, and family will help to nurture this young man to be more than a symbol of lost possibilities, through education, communication, self-resilience, assurance, and possibilities built on trust from family and himself...

As I strive to take a boy to a Man.

Excited By….

Elevated by your love,

intrigued by your grace,

excited by your presence and sweet embrace

Your spirit shines through like the stars up above, like the

stars forever in heaven is how you will be loved

Fabulous

Strong in mind and heart,

Beautiful is your spirit and essence,

Sexy is your body and passion,

in everything you touch.

In a word; you're fabulous.

Family

They come in many shapes, sizes, and colors

Each has a representation of one another

Family...

Generation to generation there always seems to be

faces, characteristics, and memories of relatives we once

knew

Family...

Side by side,

way across town,

different States,

eastside, westside, neighborhoods change,

but it's all good.

Family...

Highs and lows,

rights or wrongs,

he said, she said

would of, should have, could of,

never last long,

for some way we always seem to get along

Family…

First I love you, then I don't,

talk to you, then I won't

cry with you, cry for you

laugh together, fight together,

this is what we do

Family…

It is said that you can pick your friends but not your family

I believe from heaven above, I chose a family full of love

I'm glad to say, my best friends are my family,

Each and every one

Farewell

The music is fading and coming to an end.

No more be-bops or beats to be heard

It has brought us joy and pleasure

Touched out hearts in a way that is only special to us

But one by one the instruments exit.

Horns, strings and percussions

With a thunderous boom... all are silent!

The song is finished

Left behind is the memory that will forever be cherished...

In our hearts and mind

Farewell, old friend

I loved you from the beginning

Until the very end.

Grateful

An expression from the heart
It encompasses all the love we have and share

Grateful;

About the hopes and dreams,
Love and spirituality
Life and family, circumstances that make us be

Grateful;

Today for the possibilities that tomorrow can bring through
prayer and trusting, believing and holding on

Grateful;

For the life, love and spirituality that you inspire and pull
deep from within me

Grateful;

That you are my blessing, life and love
God's gift from above…

Grateful.

Greatest Love
"Message to Him"

Your greatest love yet you said I'm to be,

Trail and tribulations have brought you to me,

Divine interventions gift you see to reveal your destiny.

Satin blue draped on me in the morn, while breakfast was

made your eyes adorn.

Loving so good, a second time nice with satisfaction in your

smile and the gleam of your eyes.

The words we speak no longer just talk, now plans of our

future and preparation of the walk.

Hearts ready to be given for the other to entrust, leaping out
on faith we've decided we must.

Daily we work it and daily we pray, our faith in HIM
brought us and he will never lead us astray.

Through the windows of your soul,

Through the depths of my mind lies more than just
answers....

Lies love and truth clearly defined.

Greatest Love
"Message to Her"

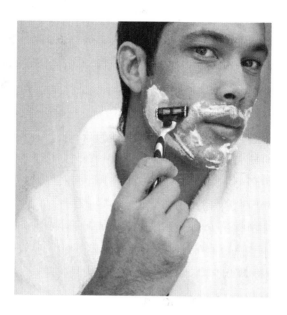

Remembrance of our morning still on my mind and vision
of satin blue so divine.

Conversation, breakfast and sweet melodies elevate our
sexual escapade energy.

As I reflect about all that we hope and have, know this my
sweet…..

You are my Greatest Love!

Guiding Life

Awake in the morning and memories of yesterday fill my mind, questions, answers, laughing, crying.... Family love consumes my very soul.

Precious little gifts with stories yet to be unfold, adolescent man his direction to be mold.

Unity of you and me with our desires only for the best, praying our paths have been heaven blessed.

Trusting, believing that it will all come to pass, unified spirits, family, love and success all in one household and each... has been blessed.

HIS Word

Let me be the first to send the daily rhyme to thank you for
HIS word and much needed spiritual time.

At first I was unsure, thought our religions would clash,
then I remembered HIS word was written for all a righteous
path.

Choose however ye to worship, acknowledge HIM and give
praise for he provided all the answers... for every question
man could raise.

We share HIM when together, we share HIM when apart,
sharing HIM today PSALMS 139...

"The Prayer of a Believing Heart"

Believe wholehearted, the trinity does save, believe
wholehearted, our union through the last days.

R.C.B.

What Could Be...

Thoughts of you are a cascade in my mind,

Bodies of two, becoming like one.

Dreaming with possibilities of what could be, me loving

you, you loving me.

Day by day closer we draw spiritual, family, friends, love

who knows how far.

True divine wisdom is guiding our paths, greater gifts GOD

has for us to have.

Moving forward with GOD's grace and trust, knowing this

is love and not lust!

Pillow Top Tears

Nighttime, pillow top tears of hope, desires, fears.

Realization from your mind as two hearts beat in sync,

how divine.

Pillow top tears hold inside the true essence of what been

long desired; life, love, trust, unity of you, me and family.

Ecstasy fades into sleep until we awake in a heat, a heat that

now burns away most of our concerns, opening to another

trust of a deeper kind.

Sensual escapade, rapture so sweet, musical moans to a

jazzy beat; bliss achieved… quenching, drenching and

erasing… Pillow Top Tears.

I Fell

I fell for you, you fell for me, a chance meet now with
possibilities,

Start to now a path unsure, but we find ourselves knocking
on love's door.

Day by day time well spent draws us closer to our hearts
content.

Trust, love and spiritual growth too… Life's long realities
begin to come true.

So down this road I gladly walk with you,

Leading, loving, guiding, supporting in all you do

I have

God give me assurance through following his word and
keeping the faith
You give love and compassion that inspires me and gives
me strength
Our family helps me stand when the way gets rough
Keeps me focused on all the blessings
God has given us
Unity, love and growth is what I cherish everyday
Thank you God,
Thank you family…for making my life just great!

I See

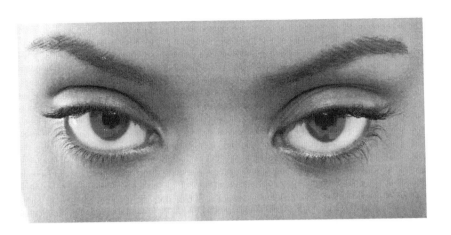

Your physical is beautiful and your mental infinite,

Your heart and soul transcends it all.

There is a deeper prize that shines through your eyes,

It's your true spirit that I See.

I Wish...

I wish you enough sun to keep your attitude bright.

I wish you enough rain to appreciate the sun even more.

I wish you enough happiness to keep your spirit alive and everlasting.

I wish you enough pain so that even the smallest of joys in life may appear bigger.

I wish you enough gain to satisfy your wanting.

I wish you enough loss to appreciate all that you possess.

I wish you enough hellos to get you through the final good-bye.

I wish you enough dreams to lead you to your goals.

I wish you enough challenges that push you to new levels.

I wish you safe, happy seasons sprinkled with rest, relaxation and rejuvenation.

Love Is

Each day I love you more,

Today more than yesterday and less than tomorrow,

For love, symbol of eternity, has no sense of time

It destroys all memory of a beginning...

And all fear of its end.

Missing You

All day in my mind, I've been missing you
The sunshine from your smile,
the loving peace in your eyes,
I've been missing you.
All day in my mind, I've been missing you
That voice that elevates & builds,
that's never destructive or negative,
the embrace from heaven which is the calmest of all my
storms... Serenity, I've been missing you.
All day in my mind, I've been missing you
Spirit touched from up above
gives increased wisdom, love, and charity
that can only be matched by the angels above
I've been missing you.
All day in my mind, I've been missing you
Hand in hand, I dream of the time
that we will forever be united in love under one trust,
honoring and HIS holy words....
I've been missing you.

Dare To Love

In my pursuit for happiness to my surprise you stood,

inspired me and dared me to love, though I said I never

would.

Some will chase, the smartest of them will keep a steady

pace,

You & I both know that no greater love can be found, we're

too far ahead in this race.

A blessing called you, a blessing called me

This is what HE gave to us to share and for the world to

see...

Both reaping the benefits

From honor, trust and loyalty.

R.C.B.

Today
"Tribute to Dr. Martin Luther King"

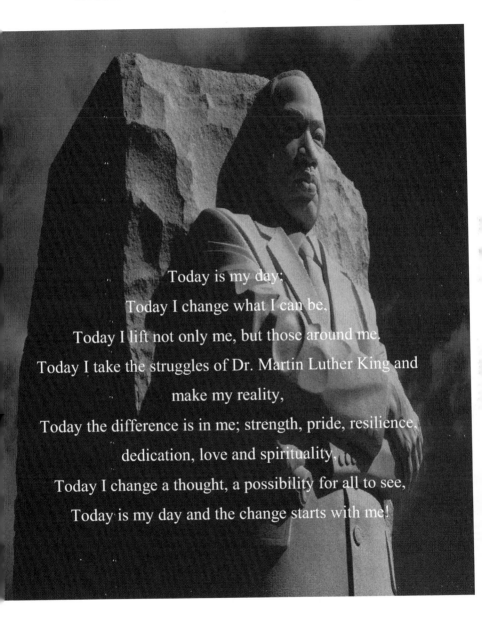

Today is my day:
Today I change what I can be,
Today I lift not only me, but those around me.
Today I take the struggles of Dr. Martin Luther King and
make my reality,
Today the difference is in me; strength, pride, resilience,
dedication, love and spirituality,
Today I change a thought, a possibility for all to see,
Today is my day and the change starts with me!

Watch
by Sarah H. Stewart

Watch your Thoughts;
they become your Words.

Watch your Words;
they become your Actions.

Watch your Actions;
they become your Habits.

Watch your Habits;
they become your Character.

Watch your Character;
it becomes your Destiny.

Why I Love You

Why I love you so... Is it your smooth chocolate texture or your true essence that lives within? Is it that you could be the standard of beauty?

Why I love you so... Is it the melodic tone of your voice? The power in your touch? How everything is forever changed and enhanced? Is it the creativity of your mind?

Why I love you so... Is it the majestic, soulful, dignified manner that you project? Is it your poetry in motion, with every step, that sends vibrations to my core?

Is it the value I find hidden deep inside,
that simulates my mind?

Why I love you so… Is it the physical or the mental,
temporal pleasures or soul mate treasures? It's funny how
both can exist in the same space and time, yet our love
continues to blow minds.

Why I love you so… Is it that our souls are consumed by
possibilities, divine intervention of what was never to be? Is
it growth, strength, passion, desire, and achievement that
fuels our fire… for life, love, family, spiritually & success?

Why I love you so… Is it because love
has no rhyme or reasons?

Why

I

love

you

so…

Chocolate Dream

Dark sexy chocolate dream… from the beginning to infinity
our souls have seem to unite our paths in a way that only
others can dream
Dark sexy chocolate dream… You have proven to be the
very best of everything a man could hope and dream,
making our fantasies become reality with God, love, life and
family
Dark sexy chocolate dream… my lover, partner, friend, the
life force from within, the true gift from above entrusted to
me to love
Dark sexy chocolate dream… Love you I will, love you I
must, for to love you is to breath and without breathe, there
is no life
Dark sexy chocolate dream…You have challenged me to be
all that a man should be; Lover, partner, father, mentor,
supporter and friend… for you, I and family,
My dark sexy chocolate dream

Morning Bliss

Morning bliss, anticipation in our minds and sensual escapade of epic proportion is about to go down

Desires turned into passion finds our bodies drenched from this morning bliss.

Reflecting thoughts of how sweet it was, is, and can be; the life, love, and dreams we share
So as we take this path to a new height
let us always remember,
Morning bliss…

My Gift

Representation of life, my destiny

My hope on a stormy sea

The peace that calms my fears

The voice that's music to my ears

My light that guides me in darkest days

But of these things that I know to be true,

my gift from God, is how I will always love you

Night Gifts

Music, writing, reading and the excitement of gifts fill the room...

In the night, silent mode; love making that climbs higher and higher until our ecstasy explodes.

Late night treats to regenerate our fuel; we sleep then wake up to start anew. Morning bliss achieved and we're running late, all our needs met we realize this loving is so great.

Loving so great this my partner can say, moans in early morn give us away. The gifts received fueled our passion indeed, but a place and a time is really all we need!!

Sitting here throbbing, flashbacks fills my head I'd trade that in an instant for a replay instead...

Freedom of expressions from our passionate encounters, the rush of your climatic thrust enhances the serenity of your sultry soul which embraces and compels true emotions shared to come alive.

Passion From Within

The best and most beautiful thing about this day cannot be

seen or touched,

It is felt from the energy,

Passion and desire from you,

With the serenity of your voice,

The power of your spirit makes your total beauty Shine

through like a diamond in the sun.

Recognized

Two minds alike to share one heart to me once was the
scary part.
Now with all the time, loving and talks my eyes now see
that special walk.
A walk you took three times before, a walk three times I'd
shut the door.
We both have grown and been set free to fulfill our true date
with destiny.
If your smiling, blushing or have butterflies, your love for
me has just been recognized.

R.C.B.

Revelations

The world around me:
Every day I see crime, drugs, violence and poverty
Has this become our living reality?
Who among us cares? As long as it doesn't bother me!

The world around me:
Those in power powerless to help themselves
So there's no help for me.
Once talk of change, fades to silence,
Back to status quo
No one remembers the little folks.

The world around me:
Tidal waves, earthquakes, fires, floods, global warming
What does it take?
God is watching
Even He can only stand so much
…Revelations.
The world around me:

Noticing the shadow of darkness

Covering the earth and consuming the human race

The shadow represents Evil, and grows at an alarming pace.

The world around me:

Wake up! Stand up! Step up!

With voices and hands in prayer,

Before it's too late and the world is silent.

Forever!

The world around me:

Realize that the same hope that built a nation from slavery

to Presidency

Is the hope we need to stand out now!

Pray and have the Audacity to Hope!

World, around, me...

Shared Moments

Great was the time with friends last night,

To home we go to sleep and hold each other tight.

Morning came up and I went down...... Oh the joy of your

sexual sounds.

Now apart and off to work we go, with thoughts of the

morning, damn we wanted more.

As night comes again, desire, excitement, and passion of

what was, is now the ecstasy of you and me

Shining Star

Smooth skin that smells so sweet

Eyes like diamonds so beautiful and mystic

A sunshine smile that brightens my day

One gentle brush of your fingers, and life's okay

A warm summer night is the embrace of your arms

Soulful, beautiful, and majestic

You are a shining star

So Sexy...

With compassion soft as a cloud
You create a deep desire that will never fade away,
For it fills my soul with joy

So Sexy...
Being held in your embrace,
Giving energy that makes me feel powerful and fearless
As a lion...

So Sexy...
The passion shared with you, like a volcanic eruption
Bursting and overflowing

So Sexy...
Love, tender and true,
Like a rose in full bloom
Beautiful...

The Plan

Morning talks planning what will be,

you, me, work and the family.

Passion untouched restraint was the key to fuel greater

excitement between you and me.

This path we've chose grows and grows closer to our

destiny, from just living to true loving is how we plan to be.

So with GOD first and all our trust, we'll last til the end of

the earth.

Phenomenal Gift

I know that you are heaven sent, because I hear angels when
you speak,
When you look at me, I'm captured by your vibe and your
touch fills me with excitement and energy; I forever want to
be in that embrace.
As I gaze at the physical outside, I see glowing from inside,
your true beauty, that spirit that can't be denied,
Breath taken away, I must say as I realize… the phenomenal
gift from heaven that you are.

Superstar

Young or old;

Blessed to have grown strong in mind, body and soul every

step of the way, today we celebrate your life with words and

praise…

Happy Birthday Superstar!

For being the mother that you are; provider, maintainer,

supporter and advisor, for giving your all…

Happy Birthday Superstar Mom!

For being the friend that can be called upon at a moment notice, who's there by your side through thick and thin; advisor and comforter to the end...

Happy Birthday Superstar Friend!

For being the best lover, partner and friend a man can have, for sharing your hopes and dreams of family, love and life, to growing spiritually and nourishing our desires and possibilities to one day be the reality of all that our hearts dream...

Happy Birthday My Superstar Lover, Partner, Friend!
May God above continue to increase your heart desires, through your faith and love of HIM and the love and support of me...

Arise

Arise, arise with hearts and minds focused on God's Holy
words; it fills us with the hope that will guide us through
our day.
Physically we pray, spiritually we give, loving and trusting
while trying to do HIS will.
We walk in love, assurance and peace elevating each other
in our hopes, dreams, family, love, possibilities as we grow
stronger spiritually.

Have a Nice Day

Have a day that brings something empowering, heartfelt and more productive than yesterday, take the love that God and I have for you and make it grow!

There's Life

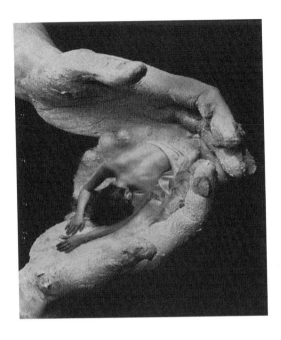

The very beginning as a heavenly blessing bestowed, even
before we had a womb to grow…
There was Life!

Nourished with love; before we had knowledge, voice or
face, before we could crawl, walk, run or talk, the
expectations of previous generations now lay on us…
There was Life!

Growing; we're giving every possible chance, love, understanding, protection, direction, education, proclamations, aspirations, spirituality and determination to become the best of what they had hoped for... In them....
There was Life!

Never stopping to ponder "why not me", adolescence and reality can be obscured; for all the love, hopes, dreams shared by those who desired us to achieve, fate, circumstances and worldly influences plays advocate too...
There is Life!

Adult: full of life and possibilities, take the path to nowhere or carry the weight of a dream?
Accept or make change, live or be lost, leader or follower, stand up or stand aside; make your choice, I've made mines, motivated by the expectations of previous generations, I hold my head up high as I choose to rise above the weight of their dream...
This, is, Life!

Thoughts of Me

I love you not for what or who you are,

but for what I am when I am with you.

When you smile and say "hello",

I have the best feeling in the world.

I know, that even for just one moment,

I have crossed your mind.

Three Words

All day busy at work, how the day just flew by with
lingering thoughts of you,
and the love we made last night.

'Twas yesterday I first heard three words from your own
lips. It raised the hair on my neck, curled my toes, and
tingled my fingertips.

The three words I once heard, said once or twice before,
to hear them come from you. The meaning… oh so much
more.

In a soothing hot bath to relax my analytic mind.
Not enough Red Cat wine to help me unwind. My own
tongue was caught, not by the Cat, but by the man I resisted
as a matter of fact.

A night of passion followed; it was sheer ecstasy.

First it was spoken, now an enacted fantasy. Not one time, not twice, but a third time around with each session; magnifying deep emotions into sound.

Intensified momentum, orgasmic release, exhaustion, and fatigue; we're in it knee deep. No whimpers or whines, no misery; only loud moans...

He's got me caught up; this man is bad to the bone

He loves me so much, that it was damn near gone

This love we're making is from three words cultivated,

from HIS blessings poured down,

and we're both deeply elated!

R.C.B.

You Are

The very essence of beauty is what shines through, so
loving, affectionate in all you do.
Mind so strong, heart of gold, spirit touched by God; this we
both know.
Life characteristics and attributes make you so unique that
no adequate words can explain your strength, but for all
your strength and pride, deeper inside is your greatest prize
and it makes you wonderful and beautiful.

I AM

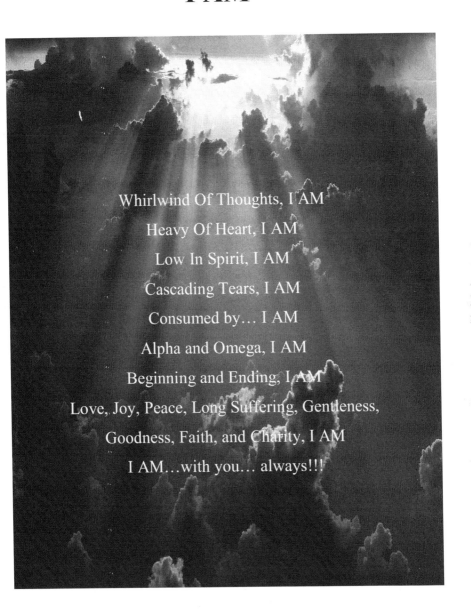

Whirlwind Of Thoughts, I AM

Heavy Of Heart, I AM

Low In Spirit, I AM

Cascading Tears, I AM

Consumed by… I AM

Alpha and Omega, I AM

Beginning and Ending, I AM

Love, Joy, Peace, Long Suffering, Gentleness,

Goodness, Faith, and Charity, I AM

I AM…with you… always!!!

Truly Touched

Truly touched; by the melodic tone in her voice, her very stance reads self-assurance, her walk as she passed him by sensual sensations in motion.

Truly touched; her beauty that seems to illuminate a dark room blinding, captivating; and she is all I see, Truly touched; from her head to her toes, I realize she's not just a physical form as I experience her confidence, intrigue, excitement, and intelligence.

Truly touched; by what was never planned, two strangers that become friends, friend to lovers, lover become partner for life and family.

Truly touched; by what has come to be through faith, hope, trust, love, fate, and intervention as we share blessings yet to be received, spirituality, love, family and possibilities; heartfelt desires to be our reality.
Truly touched

Unity

Temporal transfers excitement for our minds

Spiritual uplifting is refreshing and divine

Life sometimes can be rough

Through it all, In God We Trust

Unity in all things is what we'd like to achieve

Strength through the spirit, is how we'll succeed

Life, love, and happiness we share every day

I cherish you, as God's gift, from above in every way

What A Woman is

Soft skin,

soulful,

majestic,

dignified,

attractive,

physically and mentally beautiful; you exemplify,

What A Woman is.

Happiness,

peace,

love,

freedom,

wisdom,

understanding,

passion, and compassion; these are just a few titles that

make you…pure ecstasy.

What A Woman is.

What I Like

What I Like… is your silky smooth skin and the force within

What I Like… is your true essence that reflects the standard of beauty

What I Like… is your creativity, which becomes a work of art, with everything you touch

What I Like… the energy, vibe, peace, and certainty
Poetry in motion: beautiful and mystic as only you can be

What I Like… are the hidden treasures
Not the transparent surface image before my eyes, but those
that speak in volumes from the depths of your heart and
mind

What I Like… is every moment made with you

Where Do We Go?

Where do we go from here?
Constantly we have surprised each other with love, support
and spiritual growth reaching depths within our hearts that
we could spend a lifetime giving back.
Where do we go from here?
When you trust and know that paths have been divinely
intertwining drawing us closer to what HIS will shall be.
Where do we go from here?
Take my hand, trust your heart with mine and let's become
uplifted far beyond our hopes and dream… For eternity.

Fade to Black

From a slave ship floor I look above and darkness is all I see. Now in a faraway land my culture and language has been stripped from me. No one understands the anguish inside of me.

From sunrise to sundown I work to receive no pay. Sometimes beaten, this is just there way. Raping of our women, lynching of our fathers, killing of our children... My lord and savior will justice and righteousness ever prevail?

MLK marched for equality until they bombed our churches and silenced his voice. Malcolm X used any means necessary, to balance the rest, as they water hosed us down and let their dogs do their best.

Last to be hired, first to be fired; all while carrying them on our backs as the economic divide grows at an alarming rate. Paying the highest rent in the best slums have to offer.

Narrowing the opportunities because of where we come from; with dilapidated schools... education is NOT on the rise. Selling dope is now the best business in town. Jails and cemeteries overrun with the broken dreams of a black reality.

So men stand up and stand firm. Be the leader you always wanted and needed in your life. Give back more than you receive.

Women be the mothers, teachers providers, and supporters GOD meant for you to be. Together, be Parents, our children aren't our friends. Look back at that slave ship and remember... before all of our feet and necks are shackled again.

I Have

GOD gives me assurance through following his word and keep my faith

You give me love and compassion that inspires and give me strength.

Our family helps me to stand when the way gets rough, remembering to stay focus on all the blessing GOD has giving to us.

Unity, Love, Health, Growth in Spirit and Mind are the things that I've learned to cherish every day

Thank you for what I Have and for what I don't....

For I Have a life that's great.

Know Thyself

Some believe in luck. They wait for that one moment in life to be giving as a badge of honor so that they may show their greatness.

Some believe in cause and effect. They strive daily, pressing forward, struggling to change and challenge their circumstances; elevating themselves to bring about an altered cause with a positive effect.

Some believe in hopes and maybes. They hope this or that will happen or maybe when I or maybe could you... forever, neglecting, to realize, that they are what they repeatedly do.... Nothing.

Some believe in determination; that inner drive that cries out to be heard, seen, proven, and never stopping. They realize that through dedication, energy, and persistence they can conquer all of life's obstacles.

The difference between each of us is the level in life each of us desire to be. The choices we make, guide us to whom we aspire to become. When we face what we truly believe about ourselves, and each other, we may just surprise ourselves.

Love's Surprise

Excitement, intrigue, passion is shared with every glance,
thought and moment captured with you.

Burning desires fueling, elevating each other with every
taste, touch, thrush as ecstasy engulfs with each experience.

Hearts giving freely promising only a delight that is held
within, somehow always achieving more is the wonderful
moment to be cherished over and over again.

Life can bring many things our way joys, tears, fears and
pain but through them all we listen to the synchronized
beats of our heart and found love.

Serenity

Serenity is firm and strong like an ancient rock, more beautiful than any others serenity has no peers.

Serenity is unique like that star that shines on the horizon, a shimmer of perfection. Marvelous and seductive with her ample mounds and arms more splendid than gold to be held by.

I catch a glimmer of her beautiful thighs and legs flowing without effort, and I am mesmerized with every graceful stride.

Hypnotized by her essence which seems to surpass all other things in this world in sweetness, for she is sweeter than honey when she opens her mouth to speak and her voice gently echoes over the waves of love into my very soul... inspiring me with a passion that gives me strength.

Serenity is all that I envisioned her to be, my seductive goddess, my serenity.

Strengths

Looking into the window of your soul, I see the excitement of life, and all its possibilities waiting to be unleashed into reality.

Spoken truths are revealed in your voice; past, present, and future desires that have forged the essence that is you.

Expressions of compassion felt from your heart create an atmosphere around those who are fortunate to behold. Love, Family, Friends, and Life is elevated by the inner beauty that is you.

Swaying, bending, withstanding like a mighty oak in the wind; existing through all that life has to give and has giving; forever stretching forth your limbs toward the heavens from which your nourishment comes.

Your strong spirit shines through in all that you represent and how you are rooted. I'm glad to be sharing this growth with you.

Urban Thought

In the midst I sit admiring what is called the American Dream, but the direction of my dream is not very clear. In my dream, life's reality is the poverty that is consistently engulfing and suffocating the very life force from my being.

As a reflection of you, I am that image that you ignore: a homeless man on the street that has no worth; a deliveryman or clerk at the store; a man in the crowd with no plan just hanging on the corner addicted to booze, drugs, or worst... These sub-human perceptions you see are not the real me.

Upon a closer inspection you will find that I am filled with the same thoughts and desires that motivate you. Education would be my friend, because knowledge is power. A family to give me love and support, a home to share and nourish my family in serenity.... Success.

On the surface you say that I have nothing. I am nothing because I don't look like you or have what you have. I am nothing because all I have is the poverty stricken society that is my reality.

Realizing that life has more to offer, will someone take a chance on fate or trust in a system that is so detached from those it's designed to help? And as they look at the reflection they ask, "Who will help me achieve the American Dream, or must I go on living this Urban Dream?"

Weary

I am tired and the weight of the world allows me no rest. If only for a moment of peace to close my eyes and sleep.... The world would rest with me.

My vision is sometimes obscured by the challenges I face as they come from behind me or stare me right in my face. Is this the reflection of what will be? Kneeling before the creator, I pray for the world to release me...

Into the darkness alone with a perfect reality from my mind, for in the shadows of darkness I am at peace recognized; loved as though I was in the womb of life.

Never stopping to realize in this dark reality that there is only the destruction of what could be. No horizons that can be seen; deeply engulfed in this world and its darkness.... Has this become my destiny?

What Will Matter

Someday it will all come to an end. There will be no more sunrises, no more minutes, hours or days.

All things you have collected whether treasured or forgotten will pass to someone else. Your wealth, fame and temporal power will shrivel to irrelevance. It will not matter what you owed or what you were owed. The grudges, resentments, frustrations, and jealousies will finally disappear. So too your hopes, ambitions, plans and to-do-list will expire. And the wins and losses that once seemed so important will fade away. It won't matter where you came from or what side of the tracks you lived on at the end. It won't matter whether you were beautiful or brilliant, even your gender and skin color will be irrelevant. Then how will the value of your days be measured?

What will matter is not what you brought but what you built, not what you got, but what you gave. What will matter is not your success, but your significance, not what you learned, but what you taught. What will matter is every act of integrity, compassion, courage or sacrifice that enriched, empowered or encouraged others to emulate your example of competence and character. What will matter is not how many people you knew, but how many will feel a lasting loss when you're gone. What will matter are not your memories, but the memories that live on in those who loved you. What will matter is how long you will be remembered and by whom and for what.

Living a life that matters doesn't happen by accident, it's not a matter of circumstance, but a matter of choice.

Please choose to live a life that matters...

Silhouettes of the Soul

50825057R10068

Made in the USA
Charleston, SC
09 January 2016